Success
To a
't'

How writing 10 Minutes a Day

Can Change Your Life

Praise for "Success to a 't'"

I have been using handwriting as a tool for several years now, and find it really a fantastic help in personal development.

I received a copy of **Success to a 't'** and immediately tried out the concept.

It is so simple to apply, it took no time at all to get into the flow with it, and I found it did everything is says it will do.

So simple, so special.

Rhia Jones, Cardiff, UK

Success to a 't':
How writing 10 minutes a day can change your life

Contents

Success to a '**t**':
How writing 10 minutes a day can change your life

Introduction

If I could convince you that one simple letter – one very simple letter of the alphabet – could help change your life...

And it only takes 10 – 15 minutes a day, and not necessarily every day...

Would you be interested?

I hope so, because that is indeed the truth.

In this short book you will learn:

- ✓ what it is
- ✓ what it does
- ✓ how it does it
- ✓ and how to use it to help attract whatever you want into your life.

It is a powerful tool that will get you and keep you on your way faster, with more focus and more confidence. Here is how.

Success to a 't':

How writing 10 minutes a day can change your life

Body Language and Feelings

You already know that how you act can affect how you feel. We all do.

For example:

If you choose to go around all day deliberately glum, sad, frowning and dragging your feet as you walk…

If you never smile, or laugh and physically turn your back on everyone – do you think that will affect your mood in the short term?

Obviously it would.

Do you think it would affect attitude if you keep it up till it becomes a habit?

You bet it would.

You would be the glummest, saddest, grumpiest person on the planet, with a permanent frown etching into your face more and more as the days wore on.

No beauty cream in the world could overcome that.

Or, to look on a much more positive side this:

What if you went around all day with a big smile on your face, greeting everyone with friendly warmth, perhaps a hug where appropriate, walking with a spring in your step?

What if you kept that up until it became a habit?

Do you think that would that affect your mood in the short term and your attitude in the long term?

Again, you bet your boots it would!

In fact using body language to affect feelings is often used by medical professionals and hypnotherapists when they instruct patients to concentrate on their breathing to create a more relaxed state.

Nurses often work with patients who are having trouble sleeping, by telling them to just concentrate on their breathing.

By doing so it stops them thinking of other things and the steady rhythm is soothing and relaxing.

This is an excellent example of body language affecting feelings and thought.

So body language affects how you feel just as how you feel affects how you act.

(If this concept interests you, google "Amy Cuddy." She is a very well-known authority on this topic.)

Success to a 't':

How writing 10 minutes a day can change your life

From Feelings to Attitude

Body language affects how you feel in the short term. And if the same body language is repeated over a period of time it becomes a habit: a habit of how you act and consequential habit of how you feel.

A habit of how you feel is usually referred to as an attitude. So how your move, i.e. body language, eventually affects your attitude and feelings.

It works in either direction: your feeling can cause your body language, and your body language can cause how you feel. It just depends upon which is stronger and more persistent.

The exercises in this book are designed to let you choose your body language and then make it stronger and more persistent than any mind set you presently have, so you will gradually change your feelings to match the body language.

Success to a '**t**':

How writing 10 minutes a day can change your life

Changing a Habit

It takes 21 days to break a habit.

It takes approximately 30 days, from the start, to develop a new habit in general.

If the new habit is very strongly different from your previous habit it may take a bit longer.

However, by two months of training your body and mind the new habit should have become part of you, no matter how opposite it is to your previous habit.

Success to a 't':

How writing 10 minutes a day can change your life

Handwriting as Body Language

When you write by hand you are moving your body.

Therefore it is body language. We do not always think of writing as body language in the same way we consider other movements as body language. However it is every bit as much a part of it as any other movement of your physical body.

So what works for any other body language, also works with handwriting.

If you change your body language until it becomes a habit, you will change the feelings associated with the old habit. Instead you will develop those associated with the new habit.

This may be a very novel idea to you, but **if you change your writing, you CAN change your feeling, your attitude and hence your life.**

Success to a 't':
How writing 10 minutes a day can change your life

Doubtful?

Try it out

Here is an experiment you can do for yourself.

Imagine yourself being really, really angry. You are mad as fire.

Someone somewhere has done something to you that has flipped your switch and you can't recall a time you were ever angrier.

You have to truly get into the feeling here. Pretending won't work. You have to really feel angry.

Perhaps think back to a time when you did feel that way, and put yourself there, in that time again in your mind.

Keep that angry feeling churning and write out for yourself what is making you so angry.

Success to a 't':
How writing 10 minutes a day can change your life

You don't have to write much, not the whole story, just enough so you have a sample of your writing written when you were really angry.

You have to play the part. You have to feel the anger for this to work.

Just saying "OK I'm angry" without the emotion behind it won't work. Get really mad inside and let it out as you write.

Do not worry about your writing looks. Just write.

Once you have written a few lines of writing, stop. Now, let the anger go.

Relax, just let it go and return to your normal, more equable state of mind.

Remind yourself this was just an experiment, and release all the anger and tension from your mind and your body.

Success to a 't':
How writing 10 minutes a day can change your life

Probably it would be best to take a break before the next part of this experiment since it can be difficult to generate the opposite strong emotion immediately.

But once you have relaxed for a while and feel calm again, get that imagination going once more.

Only this time, imagine that you are absolutely, overwhelmingly happy, excited and delighted over some wonderful news you have just received.

It is the best possible news you could possibly hear at this time. You are overjoyed. Picture it. Feel it. Indulge in it. You feel great. You feel energized. You are on cloud nine.

Now, keeping that feeling alive and vibrantly strong, write out how you feel.

Again, you don't need to write a book, just enough to get a good sample of your writing.

Success to a '**t**':
How writing 10 minutes a day can change your life

No reason to get rid of the good feeling – the longer it lasts the better.

Once you have finished this writing, take a look at both pieces of writing you did.

Check your writing

The basic style is probably the same – "style" is unimportant here, so whether you wrote in the same "style" or not doesn't really matter.

Instead look at the individual pen strokes in your writing.

Were the angry ones heavier, more jagged, more angular, perhaps jabs and dashes? Did the lines of writing go down, straight across?

And how about the happy writing?

Does it have softer curves, a more gentle appearance? Does it all or some of it slant upwards toward the right?

Are the lower case "e"s more open, with more space showing in the loop?

Are the ending strokes, just as you take the pen of the page before starting again on another word –

are these ending strokes more gentle and flowing than in the angry writing.

Just take some time to evaluate just how different those two pieces of writing are.

If you can see no difference, one of two things is happening.

One, you didn't really get the emotion going in your imagination.

Or two, you are looking at the style of your writing instead of the individual strokes within it.

So if you want this to work for you, you may want to try it again, or perhaps wait till the emotions happen naturally in response to a real life situation, and write then.

Most people, however, see the difference immediately.

Putting it to work for you

So we have proved that how you feel affects your writing, and that your writing is body language.

And also, we proved from the initial idea where we went over about going around looking glum or happy, that your body language also affects how you feel.

We can therefore draw the conclusion that if you write in any given way, regularly (and we're only talking 10 – 15 minutes a day, but 10 – 15 minutes on a regular basis) it will, over a period of a month or so, start to affect how you feel.

Success to a '**t**':
How writing 10 minutes a day can change your life

The Success 't'

Which brings us (at last, you say) to the **Success** "t".

Handwriting analysts, of whom I am one, know which strokes are an indication of which attitudes and qualities.

In fact your handwriting shows your entire personality clearly and accurately ... but that is another story.

Accepting that attitudes and personal qualities show in your writing, by changing your writing to include the traits that would be beneficial to you, you can actually create these in your mind and in your general behavior.

Once again, for emphasis…

If you change your writing to include the strokes that illustrate attitudes and personal qualities

that you want, you can add these very attitudes and personal qualities to your habitual behavior and emotions.

In short: change your handwriting, change your life.

It took a long time to get here, but the explanation is necessary to help you realize just how powerful a tool you have in your hands when you take up a pen to write.

Success 't' Traits

So now on to see the Success Traits that are hidden in the lower case "t".

This letter is chosen because it contains and shows the most traits in the entire alphabet.

It can contain 10 different success traits.

Most people write their lower case "t" in slightly different ways within the same writing. This is very common. In fact, it is more unusual to write them all the same way.

Although 7 of the traits we are going to discuss can all be contained in one version of the "t", the other 3 require slightly different formations. So by occasionally writing your 't' in another way, you can, if you wish, include all 10 in your writing as a whole.

Success to a 't':
How writing 10 minutes a day can change your life

But to begin with we will just work with the Success 't' that contains these 7 amazing traits.

To get the benefit of the success "t" – and you will find it a very simple letter to write, whether you write in script or print – just practice using it as you journal.

Journaling is a great thing to do anyway. It relieves stress, helps you think more clearly, creates wonderful memories … and a great deal more.

Journal about what you are intending to achieve, writing always positively, and include this simple 't' to help you stay focused and to help you keep on going.

After all, if you are engaged in focused journaling to get what you want in life, which means success in some form or another, why not add to that by using the Success "t" to help you get there?

Success to a 't':
How writing 10 minutes a day can change your life

As mentioned it takes between 3 weeks in general, but may take up to 2 months, depending on how big a change you are making, to get used to the new writing strokes.

So persevere during that time and you will find it comes quite naturally to you after a while.

(**Side note:** one of the optional traits covered in this book is the trait of perseverance, so if you have having trouble keeping on going with your writing changes and your journaling, I suggest practicing adding that trait you your writing first.

Once you have it entrenched in how you feel and act is will be there to keep you going as you go through the rest of the exercises.)

There is absolutely nothing to lose here, and so very much to gain.

Coming up are the strokes that can help create the life you want.

Success to a 't':

How writing 10 minutes a day can change your life

The Success 't' illustrated

Here is the Success "t".

Isn't that simple?

You can add that to your writing, can't you?

Read on to find what secret ingredients are in this seemingly simple, basic letter.

Success to a 't':
How writing 10 minutes a day can change your life

What's in the Success 't'?

Let's break it down into its components so you know which part means what.

Positive

Firstly we are looking at just the downstroke. The downstroke is just what it sounds like – the stroke that goes down from the top to the bottom of the letter and is usually written before the crossbar.

> The straight, strong downward stroke of, what will become, a lower case 't' shows the trait of Positive

This downstroke should be firm and completely straight, starting and ending abruptly. That is, it does not fade in or out either starting or ending.

The slant can be upright or to the right. It is best to avoid a backhand (leftward) slant since this means holding in, and you don't want to hold in your success.

The attitude, the way of being expressed in this **firm, straight downstroke** of the 't' (or a similar strong, unwavering downstroke in any other letter, for that matter) is a **positive attitude.**

And here is a good place to mention that when it comes to handwriting, **not having a trait does not mean you have the opposite.**

So in this case, if you don't already have the positive downstroke in your t, or anywhere else in your writing, that does **not** mean you are negative.

Success to a 't':
How writing 10 minutes a day can change your life

It simply means you do not have that extra degree of positivity that could help you achieve what you want in life.

And now is your chance to get it, just by adding it to your writing.

Success to a '**t**':
How writing 10 minutes a day can change your life

Independent Thinking or Pride

The other difference you can find in the downstroke of the 't' is the length of it.

Is it really short, less than twice the height of the lower case letters?

Or is it about 2 – 2 ½ times the height of the lower case letters? Or is it more than that?

a) 't' less than twice the height of lower case letters in **Independent Thinking**	b) 't' 2 to 2 ½ times the height of lower case letters is **Pride**

Success to a '**t**':
How writing 10 minutes a day can change your life

Independent Thinking

a)

The t-bar is on the letter here, to make it look like a 't', but at the moment it is only the vertical stem of the letter we are looking at.

When the t-stem is **less than twice the height of the lower case letters**, as in example a), the writer employs **independent thinking**.

The independent thinker is not a rebel and does not do things just to be different.

However if this writer believes they have a better idea they are quite prepared to go against convention or established procedures to follow their own path.

Success to a 't':
How writing 10 minutes a day can change your life

On the other hand, if they agree with "what has always been done" as being best, they are content to follow along with that.

Pride

b)

Example b) shows the t-stem **2 to 2 ½ times the height of the lower case letters** and this shows **pride**.

Not the kind of pride that goes before a fall, but taking pride in themselves and in all they do. This is the kind of pride that results in anyone doing the best job they can at anything they do.

Do not go **more than 2 ½ times the height of the lower case letters**, as this is the indication that pride is getting overblown and becoming **vanity.**

You may want to keep what you have in the height of your t-stems, unless you have vanity, in which case it would be good to change it.

Success to a '**t**':
How writing 10 minutes a day can change your life

Or, you may choose to include a few of each of independent thinking and pride so you get the best of both worlds.

It all depends upon what you want. That is the goal in changing your writing: to get what you want.

Unless vanity is present, it is not a necessity to make a change.

Will Power/ Motivation

Next we will add a t-bar, or cross-stroke.

It is necessary for the t-bar to actually go across the t-stem to qualify for any of the Success traits described here.

T-bars off to the right, or left or above the t-stem – or missing entirely – remove their ability to give you the success boost you are after.

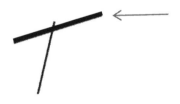

T-bar heavier than the rest of the writing shows **Will Power/ Motivation**

Success to a '**t**':
How writing 10 minutes a day can change your life

So here again is the Success 't' we've been looking at.

You already know about the downstroke, so here we will discuss the t-bar only.

First note that this t-bar is actually slightly **heavier in weight or pressure** than the t-stem. The writer has pressed harder with the pen when writing it.

This indicates depth of feeling, drive and strength. It is the indication of will power, or starting power. It shows the amount of drive the writer will employ to get going on any project or endeavor.

In the example the t-bar is only slightly heavier than the downstroke and this is fine.

However if the t-bar is even more noticeably heavier than the rest of the writing, it is an indication of even more force behind the writers ability to get started.

Conversely, a t-bar which is just a faint mark on the page, not even having the strength to form a distinctive stroke, shows someone who will have a hard time getting going on anything with any amount of energy behind them.

So if you see even some of your t-bars showing a lack of depth and pressure, start deliberately increasing the heaviness of these strokes until it becomes natural, and you will find yourself with more motivation.

This can be a tricky one to keep going with till it becomes a habit.

Because if you have light t-bars, you don't have the starting power, but you need the starting power to start working on increasing the heaviness of your t-bars…

Make it a priority, because once you have that working for you, it will be much easier to accomplish any other changes you want –

courtesy of your newly developed motivation and will power.

Goals

Next look at where the t-bar is placed on the t-stem.

> **High, Practical Goals** are shown when the t-bar is high on the t-stem

It is high up. It's almost at the top in what we traditionally use for a capital "T", but this is a lower case 't' with a high t-bar.

The higher the t-bar on the t-stem the higher the goals of the writer.

Success to a '**t**':
How writing 10 minutes a day can change your life

If you put the t-bar high on the t-stem, well above the top of the lower case letters, but still below the very top of the t-stem, then you are ambitious, but in a practical way.

However, it is to be noted that many successful people write with low t-bars.

It just means they have day to day goals and like to complete one step before considering the next one.

But to succeed more quickly, with more drive and energy, the higher t-bar will get you there faster.

T-bar balanced on the very top of the t-stem, as in a capital T, but used as a lower case letter. This shows **distant goals**.

If you put the t-bar right on the very top of the t-stem, still touching that means you stand at the bottom of the ladder of success looking up and believing that if you just go after what you want at the very top, that you can make it.

The best success t-bars are a combination of practical and the distant goals.

This brings a combination of dare-devil "one-leap-will-get-me-there" and practical "I know I can do this."

But choose which ever of the two, or combination of the two you want.

Although I have chosen the Practical High Goals for the Success 't', it is good to include a few distant goal t-bars as well.

Taking a calculated risk once in a while is good, and there is certainly no harm in reaching for the top.

Success to a 't':
How writing 10 minutes a day can change your life

So mix up your t-bars (you probably do anyway – most people have a variety.)

Just lose the low ones and the flying-in-the-sky ones that float above the top of the t-stem. Then you will have goals that will get you where you want to go.

Enthusiasm

The next two traits can be added to your budding **Success 't'** quite easily.

As you remember to make the t-stem strong and straight, and the t-bar heavy and high, the next thing to do is make it long.

Very long. The longer (within reason) the better.

This is the trait of enthusiasm.

It is an almost magical trait that sweeps everyone (including you) along with it.

Plan your plans, set your goals and go after them with enthusiasm and you are likely to achieve your dreams much faster and more successfully.

Success to a '**t**':
How writing 10 minutes a day can change your life

Enthusiasm is shown in the long sweeping t-bar

Any t-bar that is longer than the width of the average lower case letter, say an 'o', shows enthusiasm.

The 't' above shows good enthusiasm, but it could well be even longer.

Success to a '**t**':
How writing 10 minutes a day can change your life

When you write a word with two 't's together, as in 'getting' it is an opportunity to go to town on your t-bar and make it extravagantly long.

So get enthusiastic about your t-bars and find things flow much more easily in your direction.

Success to a 't':
How writing 10 minutes a day can change your life

Optimism

And that brings us to the last trait in our **Success 't'.**

You may have been wondering why the t-bars in the examples always **slant upwards to the right**.

This is to show the trait of **optimism**.

Obviously it is good to be optimistic, and by slanting your t-bars in this way you are bringing this into your writing.

Entire lines of writing slanting upwards are another indication of optimism.

So here one more time is our **Success 't'** and this time, check out how optimistic it is.

Success to a '**t**':
How writing 10 minutes a day can change your life

Upward slanting t-bar shows optimism

Here are some other examples of the use of the **Success 't'.**

cattle   wanT

TenT   about

So now you know all the ingredients in the **Success 't'.**

They are:

- Positive
- Pride
- Independent Thinking/Pride
- Strong Motivation
- High Goals
- Enthusiasm
- Optimism

Not bad for one little letter with only two strokes – and easy enough for a three year old to write.

By just adding this way of writing your lower case 't' to your writing on a regular basis, including it as you journal, you are keeping your focus while expecting success.

Success to a 't':

How writing 10 minutes a day can change your life

And a Couple More…

There are a couple of other 't's that also spell success which I will mention.

I am pointing them out so that if you already have them already you won't be getting rid of them in exchange for the t's above.

If you do have either of the two t's I am about to mention, it is a good idea to include them occasionally. It is likely you do exactly that right now as neither of them would be easy to write in every word.

But start using the Success 't' the rest of the time.

These are also written in a lower case 't' but cannot be combined with the Success 't'.

To use them you will have to just put them in at other times.

Success to a 't':

How writing 10 minutes a day can change your life

The first one is:

Persistence

Not giving up is always a good way to be.

And this stroke is easy to add to your writing as in addition to showing in a t-bar, can also show in several other letters.

It would therefore be a good idea to use it in these other letters and keep your Success 't' intact.

Notice the way the t-bar goes in an
<u>anti-clockwise</u> loop to form a knot.
This is **persistence**

Success to a 't':
How writing 10 minutes a day can change your life

It is important to check that it was written in an anti-clockwise direction, since if it goes in a clockwise direction it is not persistence.

This trait can show in other letters as shown below.

Other examples of **persistence.**

As you can see, it can be used instead of the word "and". The other letters shown here are the capital 'A', the capital 'H' and the lower case 'f'.

Success to a '**t**':
How writing 10 minutes a day can change your life

You may discover you already put this stroke elsewhere in your writing, and that is fine.

Anywhere this anti-clockwise knot appears, it shows persistence.

Success to a 't':
How writing 10 minutes a day can change your life

Initiative

This last success trait can show in a lower case 't', and ONLY in the lower case 't'. It is the trait of **initiative**.

To use your initiative means to use intelligence or imagination to get something started or to do something in a different way.

If you recall the saying "If you keep doing things the way they have always been done, you will get what you have always got."

Sometimes to be a success, you have to change your direction and do something different or differently.

If you have the trait of initiative this will be that much easier and more natural for you.

Success to a '**t**':
How writing 10 minutes a day can change your life

Initiative can only show in a lower case 't' when it is the last letter before you lift your pen from the page.

So if you print, or do a mixture of printing and script, it could be in the middle of a word but it is seldom seen there.

It usually appears as the last letter of a word.

The trait of **Initiative** is shown where the last stroke of the lower case 't' swing out energetically to the right.

Success to a '**t**':
How writing 10 minutes a day can change your life

If you are thinking it looks a bit strange, yes it does if you are thinking of schoolroom writing.

However if you start to watch for it in any writing you see, you will find it appears occasionally.

It is not a common trait and therefore all the more valuable.

You will see that the positive t-stem goes down to the bottom of the letter, forms a sharp angle and swings out with a slight curve and flourish to the right.

This is initiative.

It is not strictly speaking a t-bar, but it is in a lower case 't' and it is replacing a t-bar, so it counts for our uses.

If the curving flourish t-bar stroke is not flexible and energetic, it is not initiative.

The rigid, straight final stroke here **cannot** be considered as initiative.

The 'cat' above in NOT initiative.

Just look at the difference in the last upward directed stroke in this and the previous example.

This one is angular at the bottom, yes, (which means analytical) but there is no sweep, no flourish, no flexibility.

It is just a short, rigid stroke.

Initiative either in writing, or in life, cannot be rigid and inflexible or it doesn't work.

Success to a 't':
How writing 10 minutes a day can change your life

That concludes the list of Success traits that you might want to add to your lower case 't'

The last two, persistence and initiative I suggest you just leave for now, until you have the original Success 't' firmly established in your writing.

Then you can choose to add them or not.

But before we finish I would like to show you a few traits you do NOT want to add to your letter 't'.

I point these out so that if you already have them, or find yourself adding them at any time, you will be alerted to get rid of them again!

Success to a 't':

How writing 10 minutes a day can change your life

Do NOT allow the following strokes into your lower case 't'.

There are four of them.

The first one, if it is in already your writing, it can be very hard to remove.

I know. It is one of my problem areas and I have to work on it frequently.

It is sensitivity to criticism.

It can show in either a 't' stem or the stem of the lower case 'd'.

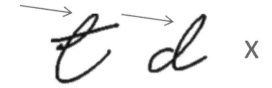

X

Sensitivity to Criticism
in shown in the loop on the 't' or 'd' stem.

Success to a '**t**':
How writing 10 minutes a day can change your life

The loop on the stem of the 't' or 'd' is the indication that sensitivity to criticism is present.

If you are writing the **success** '**t**' correctly sensitivity to criticism will not be appearing anyway.

This is because you are only making a downward stroke for the success 't'.

Sensitivity to criticism requires as upstroke followed by a downstroke to make the loop.

However, it is not so easy with the 'd' as most people write the 'd' with the upstroke of the stem coming out of the circle part of the letter, then down.

So if you have a loop there, consider whether you want to work on that, once you have your Success 't' as a regular part of your writing.

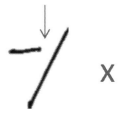

Procrastination shows in the t-bar to the left of the t-stem

The second stroke to avoid is above.

When the t-bar does not cross the t-stem, but stays to the left of it, **procrastination** is present.

Success does not usually go hand in hand with procrastination, so if you find this in your writing, it is a good idea to practice making the t-bar go right across the t-stem every time.

And it is also possible of course, to make the t-bar off to the right of the t-stem.

This is not a success trait either.

This indicates **temper**.

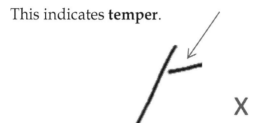

X

Temper shows where the t-bar is off to the right of the t-stem, not crossing it.

So if you see this one appearing in your writing practice making sure the t-bar goes right across the t-stem.

And the last one is not a terrible one to have appearing if it only appears once in a while.

X

T-bar floating above the top of the t-stem is the indication of a **dreamer**.

The t-bar floating in the air above the s-stem is the dreamer.

Their goals and ambitions are 'out there' to be achieved 'some time', which, unfortunately, all too often means 'never."

So if you find your t-bars up in the clouds, bring them down to earth and attach them to the t-stem.

Success to a '**t**':
How writing 10 minutes a day can change your life

Just as a little point of interest, if you find you have the occasional floating t-bar, pay attention to what you are writing about at that time.

You will probably find the vague and far distant connection with reality that the t-bar shows is also shown in how you feel about achieving or doing whatever it is you are writing or thinking about at that time.

Conclusion

And so now you know all of the traits included in the Success 't', and a couple of extra traits you can add to help you on your way.

You also know how to recognize 4 traits that can sabotage your success if you'll let them.

So I encourage you to practice your Success 't'.

As you have seen it is amazingly simple and will be just as easy to write whether you usually write in script or print.

Just keep on doing it.

3 weeks, 10 minutes a day writing out positive thoughts on what you intend to achieve is not a very high price to pay for ultimate success.

So remember that you – and perhaps loved ones who will also benefit from your success – are well worth the effort.

Success to a 't':
How writing 10 minutes a day can change your life

Practice, write, visualize the success of your goals, and keep that success 't' front and center every time your pen touches a page.

*T*o your Success

A Note from the Author:

I hope you have found this short book both interesting and helpful.

If you enjoyed the book, I would love it if you would give it a brief review on Amazon.

You can find more books on the fascinating topic of handwriting analysis, including:

- ✓ Create a Power Signature using Handwriting
- ✓ Be a Success: 10 ways to find success using Handwriting
- ✓ The Personality Analysis of your Handwriting Signature
- ✓ The Relationship Checker
    - ✓ The Happiness Course: How to become Happier

At: http://www.practical-handwriting-analysis.com
(*click on* "Handwriting Analysis Books" *on the top bar.*)

There you will also find extensive free articles, and you can contact me there also.

Success to a '**t**':

How writing 10 minutes a day can change your life

About the Author

Fiona MacKay Young has been a Certified Handwriting Analyst/ Personal Development Coach for over 30 years. She has worked with law enforcement, private investigators and lawyers. However what she most enjoys using her skills for is Personal Development.

She has written over 15 books on handwriting analysis for various uses, and also over 40 Focused Journals in which she encourages the use of the Success 't' as a tool to achieve one's goals, in addition to the power of journaling itself.

Fiona lives and works on beautiful Vancouver Island, Canada.

Made in the USA
Lexington, KY
24 November 2017